Alaska's
12 Days of Summer

Pat Chamberlin-Calamar

Illustrated by
Shannon Cartwright

PAWS IV
PUBLISHED BY
SASQUATCH BOOKS

PAT CHAMBERLIN-CALAMAR has taught everything from music and English in Denmark to folk guitar and parent-toddler classes in California. She and her husband, Don, have spent sixteen summers in Talkeetna, Alaska.

SHANNON CARTWRIGHT has been illustrating the best-selling PAWS IV children's books for more than twenty years. She and her husband live in the Talkeetna Mountains, near Denali.

Many thanks to Don Calamar, Karen Chamberlin, Susan Chamberlin, Patti Christensen, Liz Klotz-Chamberlin, Willa Michalsen, Hunter Michelbrink, Brian Okonek, Diane Calamar Okonek, Grete Perkins, Shoo Salansky, Susan Schulman, Teresa Tucker-Davies.
—P. C-C.

Blessings on all my children, step-children, grandchildren, and a great-grandchild, Haile, in far-off France.
—P. C-C.

To my wonderful brothers, Chas and Lee. Thank you for your support.
—S. C.

Published by Sasquatch Books
Printed in China
Distributed by Publishers Group West
09 08 07 06 05 04 03   6 5 4 3 2 1

Music: 12 Days. Gallic traditional (?). Original melody arrangement by Frederick Austen, 1909.
Original lyrics: Gallic traditional(?) from Husk's Songs of the Nativity, 1864.

Cover design: Kate Basart / Interior design: Stewart A. Williams / Cover and interior illustrations: Shannon Cartwright

Library of Congress Cataloging in Publication Data
Chamberlin-Calamar, Pat.
    Alaska's 12 days of summer / by Pat Chamberlin-Calamar ; illustrated by Shannon Cartwright.
        p. cm.
    Summary: Uses the rhythm of "The Twelve Days of Christmas" to introduce some animals of Alaska, from a black bear in a spruce tree to twelve Dall sheep leaping, presenting facts about each.
        ISBN 1-57061-340-0 (hardcover)
        ISBN 1-57061-341-9 (paperback)
        1. Counting—Juvenile literature. 2. Alaska—Juvenile literature. [1. Counting. 2. Tundra animals. 3. Alaska.] I. Title: Alaska's twelve days of summer. II. Cartwright, Shannon, ill. III. Title.
    QA113.C44 2003
    [E]—dc21   2002191139

Sasquatch Books
119 South Main Street, Suite 400 / Seattle, Washington 98104 / (206) 467-4300 / www.sasquatchbooks.com / books@sasquatchbooks.com

On the FIRST DAY OF SUMMER, Alaska showed to me . . .

. . . a black bear in a spruce tree.

Black bears use their curved claws to climb trees when they are disturbed or sense danger. This bear looks large, but black bears are actually the smallest of the three bear species in North America. When a black bear is born, it weighs less than a pound. But when it's grown, it weighs 125 pounds or more.

Black bears make their homes in forests, where they feed on berries, salmon, vegetation, and small rodents. A black bear's forest home in Alaska would have spruce trees, which are conifers that keep their short, green needles all year round. Other trees in the black bear's forest home might be birch, aspen, or Douglas fir.

On the SECOND DAY of summer,
Alaska showed to me
2 twin moose
and a black bear in a spruce tree.

These two moose are twins. They don't look alike because only the bull (the male moose) has antlers. He grows new antlers each spring, which drop off in the winter. Both male and female moose are very large animals, weighing between 800 and 1,600 pounds. They are also fast runners and strong swimmers. A moose can stay underwater for 1 whole minute and dive as deep as 18 feet.

Moose like to eat grasses, pond vegetation, and leaves in the summer. In the winter, they devour huge amounts of the bark and twigs of willow, birch, and aspen trees. In order to digest this woody diet, the moose has 4 stomachs.

On the THIRD day of
summer, Alaska showed to me
3 bald eagles,
2 twin moose,
and a black bear in
a spruce tree.

When these bald eagles
stretch their wings, their wingspan
can be 7½ feet long. Bald eagles live
throughout North America, but the greatest
numbers of them are in Alaska. Only the mature
eagles, those who are 4 years and older, have
completely white heads and tails.

On the FOURTH day of summer,
    Alaska showed to me
4 wood frogs,
    3 bald eagles,
2 twin moose,
    and a black bear
in a spruce tree.

Wood frogs live in
Alaska's grasslands, forests,
muskegs, and tundra. They are only 3 inches
long, and during the winter, they sleep under a blanket of dead vegetation
and snow. They can survive the long, cold winters because their body fluids turn to
sugar and freeze solid as ice. In the spring, the sun warms the tiny frogs,
thawing them out and returning them to their active lives.

On the **FIFTH DAY** of summer, Alaska showed to me . . .

5 trumpeter swans!

4 wood frogs,
  3 bald eagles,
  2 twin moose,
    and a black bear
    in a spruce tree.

The trumpeter swan is the
largest swan in the world. It's also the heaviest flying
waterfowl, weighing 22 pounds. Each year, the female swan, called a
"pen," lays 2 to 7 cream-colored eggs. Then the baby swans, called
"signets," hatch. After 15 weeks, the signets are ready to fly south with
their families to their winter feeding grounds, which range from
Cordova, Alaska, to the Columbia River in Washington.

On the SIXTH day of summer,
Alaska showed to me
6 grizzlies splashing,
5 trumpeter swans!
4 wood frogs,
3 bald eagles,
2 twin moose,
and a black bear
in a spruce tree.

Grizzlies gather on Alaska rivers
to hunt for salmon—splashing, snatching, and even
snorkeling as they try to catch the fish. Alaska grizzlies are huge:
they can weigh over 1,000 pounds. They use their powerful paws for
gathering berries, digging roots, and hunting. Grizzlies can see and
hear almost as well as humans, but they rely primarily on their
keen sense of smell.

On the SEVENTH day of summer,
Alaska showed to me
7 cranes a-dancing,
6 grizzlies splashing,
5 trumpeter swans!
4 wood frogs,
3 bald eagles,
2 twin moose,
and a black bear
in a spruce tree.

Sandhill cranes are famous for their "dance." At certain times of the year,
usually around courting season, they can be seen on the tundra, leaping, hopping, skipping,
turning, and bowing. These large cranes stand almost 3 feet tall and have a wingspan of 6 feet or
more. They migrate to Alaska's interior in mid May, where they feed on seeds, bulbs, berries, frogs, rodents,
and insects—and dance!

On the EIGHTH day of summer,
Alaska showed to me
8 mosquitoes buzzing,
7 cranes a-dancing,
6 grizzlies splashing,
5 trumpeter swans!
4 wood frogs,
3 bald eagles,
2 twin moose,
and a black bear
in a spruce tree.

Humans, bears, and caribou may not
appreciate mosquitoes, but other creatures do. Mosquitoes
provide a much-needed food source for many birds, fish, and insects.
The reason mosquitoes bite is that the female needs that little drop of
blood to develop her eggs (the male doesn't bite).

On the NINTH day of summer,
Alaska showed to me
9 salmon flashing,
8 mosquitoes buzzing,
7 cranes a-dancing,
6 grizzlies splashing,
5 trumpeter swans!
4 wood frogs,
3 bald eagles,
2 twin moose,
and a black bear
in a spruce tree.

Wild Pacific salmon may
travel more than 2,000 miles, from as far away as the
seas of northern Japan, to return to their birth-streams along the
western coast of North America. They start their long journey home when they're
ready to spawn (lay eggs). As the salmon reach fresh water, they change color and
continue on to their birth-streams to lay their tiny eggs. Then the salmon die. The new "fry," or
baby fish, develop and swim downstream all the way to the saltwater ocean, where they spend their
adult lives.

On the TENTH day of
summer, Alaska showed to me
10 caribou running,
9 salmon flashing,
8 mosquitoes buzzing,
7 cranes a-dancing,
6 grizzlies splashing,
5 trumpeter swans!
4 wood frogs,
3 bald eagles,
2 twin moose,
and a black bear
in a spruce tree.

Caribou are often called the "Nomads of the North." They travel hundreds of miles between their winter range, their spring calving ground, and their summer feeding areas. Unlike the moose, both the male and female caribou grow antlers. The male sheds his antlers in winter, while the female sheds hers in spring, after giving birth. During the summer, the caribou eat willow leaves, grasses, and flowering plants. In the winter, they paw under the snow for lichen and moss.

On the ELEVENTH day of
summer, Alaska showed to me
11 wolves a-howling,
10 caribou running,
9 salmon flashing,
8 mosquitoes buzzing,
7 cranes a-dancing,
6 grizzlies splashing,
5 trumpeter swans!
4 wood frogs,
3 bald eagles,
2 twin moose,
and a black bear
in a spruce tree.

Wolves may howl for any number of reasons: to warn intruders away, to send a message to a mate, or to find other members of the pack. If 3 or 4 wolves harmonize together, it can sound as though there are 12 or more animals instead of just a few. Although wolves live in most parts of Alaska, they are very elusive and difficult to see. They usually travel and hunt together in packs.

On the **TWELFTH** day of summer,

Alaska showed to me . . .

Dall sheep live on the alpine ridges, open meadows, and steep, rocky slopes of Alaska mountains. With their amazing balance, they can leap and climb among the high rocks and crags of their mountain home. Both the ram (male) and ewe (female) grow horns, which last their entire lives. The curling horns of the ram have ridges, or rings, that show how old he is. When he is about 8 years old, his amber-colored horns make a complete circle.

12 Dall sheep leaping,
11 wolves a-howling,
10 caribou running,
9 salmon flashing,
8 mosquitoes buzzing,
7 cranes a-dancing,
6 grizzlies splashing,
5 trumpeter swans!
4 wood frogs,
3 bald eagles,
2 twin moose,
and a black bear
in a spruce tree!

ALASKA'S **12** DAYS OF SUMMER

1. On the first day of sum - mer, A - las - ka showed to me   a black bear in a spruce tree.

2.–4. On   the   sec - ond   day   of   sum - mer,   A - las - ka   showed   to   me
            third—
            fourth—

D.S.

two   twin— moose,   and a black bear— in a spruce tree.
three   bald— ea - gles,
four   wood— frogs,

5. On the fifth day of sum - mer, A - las - ka showed to me   five trum-pet-er swans!

Fine

5.–12. four— wood frogs, three bald ea-gles,   two— twin— moose, and a black bear— in a spruce tree.

6.–12. On   the   sixth   day   of   sum - mer,   A - las - ka   showed   to   me
         sev - enth
         eighth
         ninth
         tenth
         'lev - enth
         twelfth

D.S.

six   griz - zlies splash - ing,   five   trum - pet - er   swans!
sev - en cranes a - danc - ing,
eight mos - qui - tos buz - zing,
nine   sal - mon flash - ing,
ten   car - 'bou run - ning,
'lev - en wolves a - howl - ing,
twelfth   Dall sheep leap - ing,